CULTURES IN CONFLICT:
PROBLEMS OF THE MEXICAN AMERICANS

CULTURES·IN·CONFLICT

PROBLEMS OF THE MEXICAN AMERICANS

BY DR. RUDY ACUÑA, PROFESSOR, MEXICAN AMERICAN STUDIES
SAN FERNANDO VALLEY STATE COLLEGE
AND PEGGY SHACKELTON, ELEMENTARY CONSULTANT
SANTA MONICA CITY SCHOOLS

CALIFORNIA STATE SERIES
PUBLISHED BY
CALIFORNIA STATE DEPARTMENT OF EDUCATION
SACRAMENTO, 1973

ACKNOWLEDGEMENTS

With great appreciation for Editorial and
Consultant Services to
LORRAINE PETERSON, Principal
Los Angeles Public Schools

and

ELIOT WITTENBERG, Assistant Principal
Los Angeles Public Schools

Photographs by OSCAR CASTILLO
San Fernando Valley State College

Educational Laboratory for Inter-American Studies,
Consultants:

DR. DOLORES ESCOBAR LITSINGER
MARY MARTÍNEZ
ED MORENO
DR. JULIAN NAVA

PHOTO CREDITS

CONTENTS

CHAPTER 1

Who Are The
Mexican Americans?

Every day you meet boys and girls who are different from you. Some of them are dark haired; some have blond hair. You may not have really noticed some of your friends. Does your best friend have blue eyes or brown eyes? Can you recall other members of your class that have a darker or lighter skin than you have? Did you have to think carefully about these questions? If you did, you're like many other boys and girls in America. You've learned that what a person is, is more important than how he looks.

You probably welcome the chance to talk with people who have different beliefs from yours. It's a wonderful opportunity to learn about other traditions and ideas that have been brought to America from all parts of the world. Unfortunately, not everyone has learned to accept different ideas. To understand and accept the traditions and beliefs of other people, will help us to live and work together for a better America. Read the case study about some older boys and see if you can answer the questions at the end of the story.

**LOOKING
AROUND
YOU**

Luis was doing very well in his junior year in high school. He loved his life science class and was preparing to become a doctor or a veterinarian. Suddenly his father became very ill.

Luis came from a large family and was the oldest child. When it became clear that his father could not go back to work, Luis left school. He got a job to help support his family.

One of the boys in the life science class asked, "Why did Luis quit school? I thought he was a sure winner!" Another boy replied, "So did I. He was really doing the kind of work I wish I could do. But you never can tell. Maybe he doesn't dig school. He's probably spending his time hot-rodding around town."

1. What kind of ideas did these boys have about Mexican Americans and school?

2. When the second boy said he thought Luis was different, what did he mean?

3. What were the problems Luis faced that the other boys didn't know about?

10

Part of the difficulty we have in judging other people is our lack of information about them. We may not know the whole situation. Another part is the misinformation we have built up from things we have heard or read.

This book is about people. It is about people whose ancestors lived in this country long before it was part of the United States. Some people have not understood the different way of life of the Mexican American. Because of this, it has been hard for Mexican Americans to obtain good jobs, good education, a full choice of places to live, and a chance to give their children a better life.

The student who reads this book will gain an understanding of the real situations faced by Mexican American people. If the student looks carefully and thoughtfully at the case studies, he may begin to understand the feelings and beliefs of Mexican Americans.

When differences are understood, they can be appreciated. When problems are analyzed, they can be solved. The first task of the student is to become aware. His second task is to ask himself this question. Should Juan become John? Should Juan try to keep his own culture or become like other people in the United States? Should he change his Spanish name to John and forget his Mexican heritage?

Not only Juan, but most Mexican Americans face this question. The starting point is to learn about the problems of people who have different customs and ideas from the customs and ideas of the other people around them. This book will help you to see the struggle of all Mexican Americans as they try to decide, "Should Juan become John?"

SHOULD JUAN BECOME JOHN?

CULTURE CONFLICTS

It is difficult to compare one culture with another and to decide which is "better" and which is "worse." When we try to judge the value of a culture, we need to know a great deal about the lives of the people who make up the culture. Without a great deal of knowledge, we cannot judge fairly or make a fair comparison.

We can be fair as we look at another culture if we forget the words "good" and "bad." We need to avoid using words like "higher" and "lower" and "more cultured" and "less cultured." We need, instead, to look for the reasons a culture is like it is. We need to know the customs and habits which make up the culture and the reasons why people act, think, and feel as they do. We need to see the "why" as well as the "what."

For example, someone who does not know the English language can learn little about English culture. One who does not know the Spanish language can learn little about the Mexican culture.

As another example, in some parts of the world, people have a quiet rest for an hour or two just after the noon meal. We could say that these people are lazy, or we could ask ourselves why they feel it is a good habit. In some parts of the world, men wear large hats, called sombreros, and bright ties around their necks. We can say that these men are showing off, or we could ask why they dress like that.

It is best not to make any pre-judgments at all. It is so easy to be prejudiced. We all grow up in a culture. But cultures differ. We all tend to see another culture from the point of view of the one in which we live. It is hard not to like our own ways best!

12

Boys of all ages like active sports

Working or playing, boys have fun together

The ancestors of the Mexican Americans of today have lived in this country for centuries. They lived on the land we call the Southwest long before the Anglo-American came. The term "Anglo-American" has come to mean all other white Americans who came to the Southwest. Originally, the word referred to the people of Anglo-Saxon ancestry who came to America from western Europe, particularly the English.

WHO ARE THESE PEOPLE?

Most of the ancestors of the Mexican Americans lived in close contact with Mexico. Their way of life was copied from that of Mexico. They built homes like those in Mexico and ate Mexican foods. They wore Mexican-style clothes and spoke Spanish.

Many Mexican Americans still keep many of these ways of life. It is very different from the way of life of people whose ancestors came from England, or France, or Germany. Some people do not understand the differences nor accept ways which are not like their own. That is why many Mexican Americans have had problems in living in this country.

---

1. What things do you find that are alike about these people?

2. What things seem to be different from person to person?

3. Why do you think there are differences among Mexican Americans?

4. Why do you think there are differences among your friends?

Alexander Harmer captured the spirit of the people in his painting of the early Southwest

Mexicans were the first vaqueros, or cowboys, in the United States. The Mexicans brought the first horses, sheep, pigs, cats, grapes, cotton, and olives into the Southwest. Mexicans helped to found such great cities as Los Angeles, San Francisco, and San Antonio. They added colorful and useful words to the English language and brought us their music and dancing. Men from Mexico showed us how to live on hostile desert lands.

16

Of the more than two hundred million people who live in the United States, over five million are Mexican Americans. Even though the five million all had Mexican ancestors, they call themselves by different names. In New Mexico and Colorado, many call themselves Spanish Americans, while in Texas, others prefer to be called Latin Americans. Currently, many Mexican American young people like best to call themselves Chicanos. No matter what they call themselves, they are linked through their history and their language.

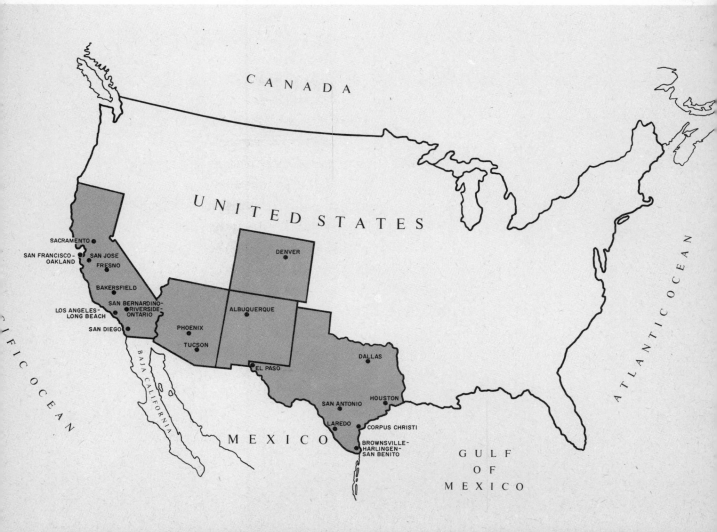

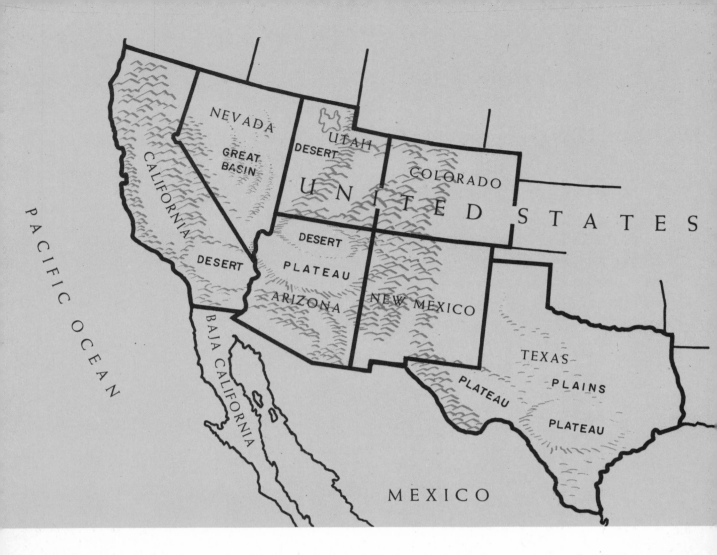

Most Mexican Americans still live in the region called the American Southwest. Though this region once belonged to Mexico, it is now the states of California, Arizona, New Mexico, and Texas. Life in these states has been greatly affected by the Mexican heritage. The history of these states is partly the history of Mexico. Their geography is most like that of the Mexican states that lie along the border. For these reasons, it has been easy for the Mexican American to keep many of his Mexican ways.

18

Maps can tell us a great deal about the Southwest. They can also tell us a great deal about the people who live in this region. See what you can find out from this map.

---

1. What kinds of weather might this region have at various times of the year?

2. What use might people make of this land?

3. What foods might be able to be grown here?

4. What kinds of clothing would people be likely to wear?

5. From what natural materials could people build their houses?

6. In what other ways would the land affect the ways in which people would live?

7. What country lies south of this region? How is that country important to those who live in the Southwest?

The desert blends into the mountains under a West Texas sky

A photograph can tell us more about the Southwest. Look at this one and answer the same questions that you answered about the map. See whether you had to change any of your answers. Use the map and the picture to answer two more questions.

1. What kinds of activities would children follow here at different times of the year?
2. What clothing would children wear in Texas tumbleweed country? At California beaches?

The tumbleweed country of Texas is much different from the urban areas of New England. This photograph of a city in New England will help you to see some of the differences. Imagine that you are a Mexican American child who has moved from a Texas ranch to this city.

_____

1. What changes would you need to make in the way in which you were used to living?

2. Which changes would be easy to make?

3. Which changes would be hard to make?

4. What changes might you have to make if you were an Anglo-American child who moved from this city to the ranch in Texas?

21

HOW DO CULTURES CHANGE?

We all grow up within a culture. We spend many years learning our own ways of life. As we grow older, we begin to learn some of the reasons behind the ways in which we live. Our own way of life becomes the most comfortable way in which to live. The things we know best and understand best become the most precious to us. We find it difficult to understand why people would want to live in any other way.

But cultures differ. Different people grow up in different ways. They learn different values and different customs. They, too, become most comfortable with the way of life which they know best. We can learn to understand the value of a different way of life by learning how a culture develops.

First, we learn the traditional ways which have been passed on to us from early ancestors to our grandparents to our parents and, finally, to us. We learn these ways first by watching and then by imitating. We listen to what older people tell us and we read what they have written. We learn our native language by listening to and imitating the sounds we hear older people make.

CASE STUDY

It has been a long day for José. He has just come to California from Texas. His name should be pronounced Ho-say', but the children call him Josie, even though Josie is more often a girl's name.

José usually understands what the teacher is saying and he usually knows the answers to her questions. His hand, however, is apt to be the last one to go up. It takes him a little extra time to think in Spanish and then put his answers into English.

1. Why do the children call him Josie instead of Ho-say? How is the letter "J" pronounced in Spanish?

2. If you went to another country that spoke a different language, how would you feel? How would you answer the teacher?

3. What kind of help can the class give José?

4. What does your school or your teacher do to help children with special problems?

23

CASE STUDY

Juan is a ten-year-old boy. He used to live in a part of the city where most people spoke Spanish. He has just moved to another part of the city where no one speaks Spanish. While Juan speaks English quite well, he does have a noticeable accent.

He enters his new school in December. All the other children have made their own friends by this time. They know what is expected in the classroom. Juan believes the other children are staring at him, so he keeps his eyes down. He thinks, too, that they laugh at him when he speaks because of his accent.

1. How do you think Juan feels when he comes to a new school in the middle of the year?

2. How did you feel when you went to a new classroom last year?

3. If you were a member of this class, what could you do about the new boy?

4. What kinds of things could you help Juan learn?

24

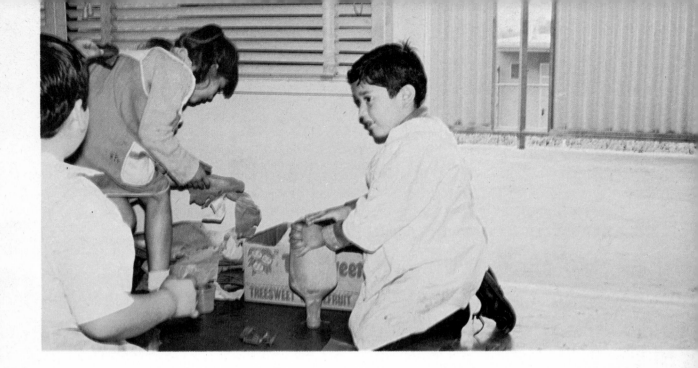

Rudy has been taught that his native language, Spanish, is beautiful. He feels comfortable speaking it because he uses it at home. On the other hand, he feels uncomfortable speaking English. His teacher insists that he speak English in the classroom and on the playground, and even urges Rudy's parents to enroll in a class to learn English.

CASE STUDY

1. If Rudy doesn't understand the teacher's reasons, what might Rudy think of her insistence on speaking English?

2. Did the teacher suggest that it was bad manners to speak Spanish instead of English?

3. Should Rudy's parents be angry at the teacher for suggesting that they learn English?

4. Why might it be difficult for Mexican Americans to give up speaking Spanish?

5. Should the whole family stop speaking Spanish?

6. How could the class make use of Rudy's Spanish?

Language is one of the important ways that culture is handed down. It can be a problem when that language is not the one people around us are using.

We have seen some imaginary situations in which the tradition of language became a problem between two cultures. In what other ways are cultures made and how do they change?

The second force that determines some of our ways of life is the land we live on. If we live in a hot and dry land, we may eat the beans which can be easily grown there. In a hot and wet land, pineapples rather than beans may be part of our diet. In a cold region, we may wear woolen clothes and caps that cover our ears. In a hot region, we may prefer cotton clothes and hats whose wide brims can protect us from the sun. Where cold weather is the rule, we may spend a great deal of time inside a large, well-heated house. Where hot weather is common, we may prefer a smaller house with a great deal of outside space.

Third, the size and makeup of our family can affect our way of life. Besides the mother and father, there may be sisters and brothers, an aunt or uncle, perhaps a grandmother and a grandfather. If we have many younger brothers and sisters, we may have to learn to take care of them. If we have no brothers or sisters, we may have to learn how to spend time alone. If our fathers are not home much of the time, we must learn to get along without them. If our fathers work at home, we will need to learn to avoid disturbing them. Some families stay in the same place year after year, while others move many times.

26

Pineapples grow in warm areas where there is a great deal of rain

Warm clothing is needed where there is ice and snow

CASE STUDY

Elena speaks English. She has never been to any school, before. However, she has many brothers and sisters with whom she enjoys playing.

While playing on the school yard, Elena is told she is in the wrong place. She should be playing on the first grade yard. Her brother, José, is in the second grade. Her sister, Margarita, is in the fourth grade. They are playing where they should.

Elena is lonely. She wants to be with José and Margarita. Every time she leaves the first grade yard, the teacher sends her back.

1. Why does Elena feel lonely?

2. What problems could there be for Elena on the yard with older children?

3. How can Elena's sister and brother help her?

28

María and her family have just come from Mexico. She doesn't speak English, although her older brothers and sisters are able to speak some English.

María's parents and her brothers and sisters love her. They give her gentle pats as she passes by. They often take her hand to help her. She loves to climb into her mother's lap for comfort. Her mother lets her do this when María is hurt or afraid or when she needs love and comfort.

María's family does not speak often or use many words. She is shy about talking. She hears the lady on the playground talking very fast.

1. What will María's first days at school be like?

2. What can her family do to help her?

3. What could you do to help her?

29

CASE STUDY

Virginia López enters Ramírez school. It is the third school she has entered this year. The land her home was on was rezoned for factories, and her family had to move.

Before this year, she had lived in one house. Now, her father and her mother must both work, and she must hurry home after school to care for three sisters.

1. When you change schools many times, what happens to your school work?

2. How will the fact that her mother has to work affect Virginia?

3. How will Virginia feel if there is something special happening after school?

A fourth change in the cultural patterns comes about because we borrow things from other cultures. Many different people in many countries watch television, for example, even though they did not invent it. As another example, many people enjoy eating Italian pizza and Mexican tacos even though their ancestors were neither Italian nor Mexican. In the Southwest, where outdoor living is common, Anglo-Americans have borrowed many words and customs from the Mexicans. The words "fiesta," "barbacoa" meaning barbecue, and "patio" describe customs which enrich our ways of living. At the same time, Mexican Americans sing and dance to Anglo-American music and watch their television programs. And Coca-Cola is as well known among Mexicans as among Americans.

Fifth, sometimes, we are forced to change our way of life against our will. This may happen because of war or a change of boundary. When Mexico gave parts of the Southwest to the United States, the people living in these areas had to live under a different set of rules and laws.

Sixth, cultures change because the people no longer need something any longer or need something else. We didn't need as many horses to pull buggies after the automobile was invented, but we needed better roads. The blacksmith, who was once a most important man, became less important. On the other hand, the roadbuilder, who had not been very important, became a very needed person. We learn to change our skills and our habits as we live in various places and work in new jobs or go to new schools.

Mexican American and Anglo-American cultures have changed as they have come in contact with one another. Sometimes, these changes have been very slow; other times, such as in the present, the cultures are changing quickly. Although Mexican Americans have accepted many Anglo-American customs, they have resisted accepting others. They want to keep many of the Mexican ways. They are proud of the ways of their ancestors. They want to keep the best parts of their own culture rather than be forced to accept Anglo-American customs that do not fit into their own way of life.

More and more roads will be needed to serve growing communities

Mission San Carlos Borromeo is an example of Mexican influence

Over five million Mexican Americans live in the United States. Though there are differences among them, certain forces have drawn them together. They have a common history and a common language. They often are living upon land that once belonged to their ancestors. Their way of life has been strongly based upon the habits and customs of Mexico. We find that they have problems when they move to other parts of the United States.

We have discussed how cultures grow and how they change. We learned that cultural conflicts come about because of traditions and language, the type of land we live on, and the patterns of our families. We found that changes came about through borrowing from other cultures, by outside forces, and through changes in needs. Through case studies of fictitious episodes, we have had opportunities to recognize the problems and offer suggestions for change.

SUMMARY

CHAPTER 2

Problems In Understanding Cultures

Every person has his own characteristics or traits. These are the things about him that make him different from his neighbor. One person may have a quick mind; that is one of his characteristics. Another person may have curly hair; that is one of his characteristics. Yet another person may speak with a lisp and throw a ball well; those are two of his characteristics.

As people form themselves into groups, the groups take on certain characteristics. A characteristic of successful students is that they do most of the work given them. A characteristic of boxing champions is that they can take a great deal of punishment.

Sometimes, all of the members in a group do not have the same characteristic. Some people with red hair may have bad tempers. This is not a characteristic of people with red hair because not all people with red hair have bad tempers.

If we think that all red-headed people have bad tempers, we are thinking in stereotypes. Once we know enough red-headed people, we know that our stereotype is wrong. A stereotype can be so wrong that it hurts everyone in the group. Nearly all of us have some stereotyped ideas. Sometimes, we do not even know that our ideas are stereotyped.

PROBLEM NUMBER ONE: OVERCOMING STEREOTYPES

37

See if you have any stereotyped ideas by studying the men in these pictures.

_____

1. Which man do you think is the most successful of the three? Why do you think so?

2. If you were a banker, to which man would you pay the most attention? Why?

3. Which man is an American? Why did you choose him?

4. Which man is a foreigner? What made you think so?

A Surveyor

A Subway Conductor

For more practice in working with stereotypes, look at these pictures.

---

1. Which of the men would have the easiest time becoming successful? Why did you choose him?

2. Which man would have the hardest time becoming successful? What makes you think so?

3. Would you change your mind if any of these men spoke with an accent?

4. Would you change your mind if any of these men showed you that he had a million dollars?

5. Describe the ways you know in which a person can be successful.

A Cartographer (map maker)

You may have found that you had some stereotyped ideas. You may have been working with opinions rather than with facts. You may not even have known that you were drawing false conclusions. Nearly every group has suffered because of such ideas. The Mexican Americans have been victims of these false ideas, too. See if you can find the ways in which Mexican American people could be hurt or kept from becoming successful in the following cases.

CASE STUDY

Mrs. Joyce Younger is an experienced teacher who has taught among Mexican American children for many years. The children like her in spite of the hard work she makes them do. Almost every night, they have homework. One of the things she makes them do is to learn about laws and the rights of individuals.

When she is asked why she works so diligently and why she has them make their own decisions, Mrs. Younger says, "The children in this class have the ability to succeed. They must work hard and set a good example for their younger brothers and sisters."

1. What might happen if these children never learned to discuss their problems, offer solutions, vote on issues, and take responsibility for their choices?

2. What would happen if Mrs. Younger said instead, "Mexican American children are happy people. I don't want to make them work too hard and be unhappy. They will just be confused if I try to make them take responsibility."

Miss Mildred Jones is a new teacher from New Hampshire. She came to the Southwest to teach. Her grades in college show that she is well prepared for her job as a teacher. When she arrived in the Southwest, she was assigned to a school in whicn almost all the children were Mexican Americans. She had never worked with a Mexican American before. She had heard that they were migrant workers and were good with their hands. She had also heard that Mexican Americans did not value an education and would probably not be successful. Miss Jones likes her students, but she is perplexed.

1. What should Miss Jones teach her students?

2. What topics would her class want to discuss?

3. How can she overcome the stereotypes she has heard about her students?

4. What difference will it make to the students whether she believes they can be successful or will probably be failures?

Sometimes people accept stereotyped ideas about other people. Sometimes, they even accept stereotyped ideas about themselves. If Miss Jones begins to believe that her students cannot succeed, her students may believe this. If she does not push her students to learn subjects they feel are too hard, they may fail the tests and begin to believe that they can never learn. The Mexican American child may feel stupid when he compares himself with other children who passed the tests. In his next class, he may not try very hard to learn. He may feel that he is already too far behind to learn very much.

Sometimes, a child does not accept a stereotyped idea about himself. He may rebel against the school, the teacher, his classmates who hold these ideas. He may feel deeply hurt and angry. To get even with these people and the school, he may try to show them that he is important by destroying or stealing things. He may write on walls or "ditch" school. He may get into trouble all the way through school. He may give up and quit before he graduates from high school. What can the other boys and girls in his class do to help him? How can the teacher and the principal help him change his self-image?

In these ways, stereotypes can be dangerous forces. Can

you think of ways in which stereotyped thinking can be avoided?

In the United States, as in other countries of the world, many differing cultures exist side by side. Each culture resembles the others, but there are many differences among them. Each culture borrows ideas from its neighbors and gives some ideas to them.

Sometimes one culture decides to give up its own way of life and join the majority group. At other times, a minority culture wants to keep its own way of life and live as it is used to living. In this event, the majority may try to force the minority to change.

The majority culture in the United States follows a way of life that began in England. We can call the members of the majority culture, therefore, Anglo-Americans. When Anglo-Americans insist that Mexican Americans change, there is often resistance. The resisters want to follow their way of life, a way that began in Mexico rather than in England. The resistance causes a feeling known as "cultural shock." We can study what this shock is like.

Anyone who is forced to change his way of life against his will can experience cultural shock. For example, if you are a girl, your family may have certain ideas about what is lady-like behavior. Your grandmother, your mother, and your sisters might believe that a lady wears dresses at all times and has very long hair.

PROBLEM NUMBER TWO: FORCING CULTURE CHANGES

47

The girls in your school may think differently. They might all cut their hair short and wear pants to school. You might very well experience cultural shock when you first come to school. The other girls might not accept you as a friend because you wore dresses and your hair was long. You might feel very upset if the girls forced you to change or if your family forced you not to change.

<table>
<tr><td>**CASE STUDY**</td><td>Eleanor's parents have taught her that it is rude for children to interrupt their elders. Her teacher, Miss Smith, wants the members of the class to join a discussion. She wants them to speak out when they have something to say. Other students interrupt one another during the discussion. Miss Smith urges Eleanor to interrupt and to speak out.</td></tr>
</table>

1. Why might Eleanor be afraid to speak out?
2. What might Eleanor be thinking about the other children in the class?
3. Why might it be difficult for her to change her behavior?

As another example, Mexican American parents teach their children to respect grown-ups. One way of showing that respect happens when a Mexican American child is being punished. He is told by his parents not to look directly into the eyes of the adult who is punishing him. To do so would be a mark of disrespect.

You might be a Mexican American boy who stayed out on the baseball field too long after recess. The teacher

48

might talk to you and insist that you look directly into his eyes while he is discussing this with you. You might not like to look directly at him because this is against your way of life. You might also be unhappy if the teacher thought you looked away from his eyes because you were a coward.

CASE STUDY

Luis has been taught to model himself after his father. His father has told him to protect his honor at all times. Losing the respect of your friends is one sign of dishonor. His teacher says Luis has done something that he did not do, and wants Luis to apologize to the class. Instead of apologizing, he argues with the teacher. The class and the teacher think Luis has no manners.

1. Why would Luis have found it difficult to apologize?
2. Why is it so important to Luis not to lose honor?
3. What would you do if you were the teacher and Luis sassed you?

PROBLEM NUMBER THREE: MISUNDER-STANDING CULTURAL DIFFERENCES

Cultural differences can become problems if we do not try to understand them. We can avoid hurting our neighbors' feelings by knowing about their way of life. We can make a special effort to understand why people wish to keep their special differences.

You already know that a culture is formed by many forces. The way each of us lives is determined by the things that have happened during our lives. It is also affected by the things that have happened during the lives of those who lived before us. As we learn from those who live with us, we

50

store up knowledge. Later, we add some knowledge of our own. We pass on this knowledge to others, especially to members of our own family.

This kind of knowledge-building is a special skill that man has. No other animal passes on knowledge in this way. Other animals teach one another, too, but they are unable to profit from the knowledge of the past. They are not taught about the things that their grandparents knew. Each animal has to learn everything over from the beginning. Only man can build upon the knowledge of other men. Men can improve their way of life by this kind of building.

The family is a good source for learning the basic facts about living. It is a good way to learn about one's own culture. It is usually the first contact a child has with his culture.

Still, as you know, all families are not alike. Since families are different, they do not teach their children the same things. Mexican American families have sometimes taught their children ways that are different from the ways taught by Anglo-American families. When the children of such families play together, there may be conflict. Bad feelings may occur when children raised one way try to force other children to do things in which they do not believe.

There are even differences among families with similar backgrounds. There are differences among Mexican American families. Much depends upon whether a family lives in the city or in the country. Much may also depend upon whether the family is rich or poor. Living in the same place for a long while may affect a family's way of life, as may moving around a great deal. Families with many children may work and play in different ways than families with few children.

We can try to understand cultural differences better by looking at two imaginary American families. We can look at them in two case studies. We may be able to see how conflict might arise between them if they came together without understanding how to look at cultural differences.

Please study the case studies on the following two pages, and answer the questions below.

---

1. In what ways are these families alike?

2. In what ways are they different?

3. What differences might not cause any clashes?

4. What differences might cause misunderstanding among the children?

5. Would language cause any conflict?

6. What differences would be interesting for the Rodríguez family to learn about the Robinson family?

7. What differences would be interesting for the Robinson family to learn about the Rodríguez family?

CASE STUDY

This is the Rodríguez family. The father, a construction worker, is named Juan. The mother, a housewife, is named Gloria. The grandmother, Dolores Romero, lives with the family and speaks no English. There are three children: María, 11; José, 12; and Celia, 8.

This is the Robinson family. The father, a television repairman, is named John. The mother, a housewife, is named Katherine. There are two children: Joe, 10, and Mary, 12.

CASE STUDY

A language difference has been one reason for clashes between the Anglo-American culture and the Mexican American culture. Many Anglo-Americans do not speak Spanish, the native tongue of Mexican Americans. Many Mexican Americans do not speak English until they begin to learn it at school.

PROBLEM
NUMBER
FOUR:
SPEAKING
A DIFFERENT
LANGUAGE

If people do not speak the same language, it is hard for them to understand one another. Learning a second language is always harder than learning one's first, or native, language. The second language may have sounds in it that the native language does not have. This makes the second language even harder to learn. Sometimes one's ears do not even hear the new sounds.

English and Spanish are quite different from one another. Many letters in the alphabet are not pronounced the same way in Spanish as they are in English. The order of words in a sentence is not the same.

Mexican American children may hear only Spanish spoken at home. They may learn no English words until they begin school. Such children may have a difficult time learning English when it is first taught to them. You can begin to see the problem by trying to learn some Spanish words and sentences.

Here is a list of some Spanish words. Column A shows the way they look in Spanish. Column B shows how they are pronounced in Spanish. Column C gives the English meaning of the Spanish word.

First, cover up Column B with a piece of paper. Try saying the words in Column A without any help. Use a tape

56

recorder if you can, so that you can listen later to the way in which you pronounced the words. Then look at Column B and say the words again. Look for the sounds you did not know and the sounds you did not hear.

COLUMN A	COLUMN B	COLUMN C
1. México	Meh'-hee-ko	Mexico
2. llamar	ya-mahr'	to call
3. mañana	mah-nyah'-nah	tomorrow
4. quiero	kee-yeh'-ro	I like
5. agua	ah'-gwah	water
6. hablo	ah'-blo	I speak
7. español	es-pah-nyohl'	Spanish
8. bien	bee-yen'	well
9. ahora	ah-oh'-rah	today
10. escuela	eh-skweh'-lah	school
11. caer	cah-yehr'	to fall
12. hola	oh'-lah	hello
13. acción	ahk-see-yon'	action
14. patio	pah'-tyo	patio
15. hombre	ohm'-bray	man
16. copia	co'-pyah	copy

How many words did you get right the first time? What sounds didn't you hear? What sounds were hard to make? How is the letter "e" different in Spanish than it is in English? What other differences did you notice? Did you come closer to sounding like a Mexican American during your second try?

Now try saying these three sentences:

1. Me llamo María.   My name is Mary.

2. Quiero agua.   I want water.

3. ¿A dónde está el escusado?   Where is the toilet?

What problems did you have? If you were in school in Mexico, you might need to know these sentences. How would you feel in that case if you did not know Spanish? What would you do? If you were living in Mexico, would you want to be taught in Spanish or in English? Why might it be best to know both languages?

Can you see now how hard it would be to live in a place where nobody knew your language? For this reason, Mexican Americans sometimes prefer to live in the part of a city where everyone knows Spanish. Would you try to live in a place in Mexico where people knew English? Would you want to learn Spanish if you lived in that place?

If you would really like to learn the words, try this way. Have someone who knows Spanish well put the words on recording tape for you. Then you can listen to them over and over and repeat them correctly.

There are thirty-two children in a fifth grade class. Six of the children do not speak English very well, though they do understand it much better than they once did. Each of the six students makes frequent mistakes.

1. Who should the teacher call on to correct the mistakes?

2. What kind of problems might the teacher cause if an Anglo-American student was always asked to give the correct pronunciation for the Mexican American student?

3. Are there certain letters that will have quite a different pronunciation in Spanish than in English? Which ones?

4. Do you think it would be difficult to answer questions in a language with which you are not very familiar?

CASE STUDY

The teacher usually puts a nice comment on perfect spelling tests. She sometimes says "Excellent," "You're doing a fine job," or "Well done." These tests are then put up on the bulletin board.

Manuel, a Mexican American boy wants very much to get a perfect paper and have his spelling test on the bulletin board with such a comment. He has shown much improvement. Six weeks ago, he was getting only eight words correct out of the 20 on the test. Now he can get 14 right. But he has never had his paper up on the bulletin board.

1. What could the teacher do to help Manuel feel a sense of accomplishment in his spelling?

2. What might Manuel feel if he never gets a perfect paper? Will he give up?

3. Should Manuel receive credit for the great improvement he has shown?

When we first look at something or someone, we form a first impression. This is our first way of thinking or feeling at that very moment. First impressions are important as we form opinions. Our whole way of looking at a thing in the future may be colored by our first impression of that thing.

Pretend that you are looking at a ragged dog who had no collar. The first thing you see him do is tip over a garbage can. You decide that he is looking for food. Which one of the following might your first thought be?

a. He is a stray dog.
b. He is hungry.
c. He is ugly.
d. He is smart to find his food this way.

61

Which one of the following feelings about the dog might you first have?

    a. You are sorry for him.
    b. You are angry at him for upsetting the can.
    c. You are afraid of him because he is not trained.
    d. You dislike him because he looks dirty.

First impressions are important. They set the pattern for how we will behave later. When we meet someone new, we get a first impression. When we go some place new, we get first impressions. Others have first impressions about us, too.

1. Did the teacher have enough background information about these children?

2. What may happen when you judge from first impressions only?

3. In what other ways could the teacher have handled this situation?

4. Do we know all the facts about the way Juan and María usually act in class from this episode? Could that make a difference in the way the teacher responded?

62

When a person or place is very different from what we are used to, first impressions become more important. A place may be so different from places in our own culture that we feel cultural shock. Our first impressions may cause feelings of fear, anger, and confusion.

Sometimes, the first day in a new school is a whole day of cultural shocks. It may be like this even if everyone in the school speaks our language. It can be worse if everyone speaks a different language.

We have been looking at some of the ways in which people differ from one another. We have seen that one person's way of life can differ from that of his neighbor. We have watched as cultures have come into conflict. We have even imagined how culture clashes might arise. We can remember these important ideas from our study:

SUMMARY

1. We sometimes judge a culture before we know all the facts and before we understand the reasons for customs and beliefs.

2. We sometimes judge all members of a group by what we know about one member of the group.

3. We sometimes force people to change their ways even when they feel deeply against changing.

4. We sometimes forget that there are differences which family members cherish and which they believe to be important enough to keep.

5. We sometimes expect people who do not understand our language to fit quickly into our way of life.

6. We sometimes judge others by the first impression they make upon us and fail to help other people overcome the cultural shock of their first impression of us.

CHAPTER 3

How Does The Past Affect The Present?

Culture conflicts can come at any time. The closer together people of differing cultures live, the more often they can come into contact with one another. The modern city houses people from many cultures. The city is a comfortable place to live, but it also offers frequent chances for clashes. It is only by understanding our neighbors that we can appreciate their way of life.

Our understanding of our neighbors can be built from many sources. We get some of our information from the older people we know. They tell us, in words or in actions, how to think about other people. We get more facts and opinions from the boys and girls of our own age. Their feelings about other cultures are important to us.

The ways in which the people we know act and think are not the only forces that act upon each of us. We are able to read many accounts of the past. We have books and newspapers and magazines that tell us what happened many years ago. We depend upon the writers of these accounts to tell us an accurate story. Sometimes the writer is not careful to tell all the facts as he spins his tale. Sometimes he does

HERITAGE OR HANDICAP?

The charro serenades a señorita on the streets of early Santa Fé

not take the time or the trouble to find out the reasons behind the actions of the people he is describing.

If a man tells a story about our grandfather, we will listen closely. We are interested because the subject of the story is familiar to us. If the story tells how great our grandfather was, we will feel proud and happy. If it tells about how he was a coward, we will be angry or sad. If we read a story about the courage and skill of our ancestors, we will want to imitate them. If the story tells something bad about our ancestors, we will feel ashamed of them.

When we read a story, we trust the author to tell us true facts about what happened. We trust him to have told us what actually took place. Sometimes our trust is misplaced. What we think are facts turn out to be only opinions. We sometimes find that the prejudice of the author changes his account of an incident in history. We often accept these accounts as true, rather than finding out for ourselves.

Some accounts that have been written about the Mexicans of the past have not been accurate. Such accounts have spread bad feelings among people who do not know the truth about the early settlers of the Southwest. We can look at one such account and judge its effects upon the people who read it. We can also look at several imaginary case studies to see why an account might have been written.

Zebulon Pike was a major in the United States Army more than a hundred years ago. He made a journey to see the Southwest with his own eyes. He described what he saw and what he thought in a journal that became popular in the East.

A traditional dancing costume combines lace and design

Major Pike was one of the first Anglo-Americans to write about the Mexicans in the Southwest. His journal describes his visit to the Mexican city of Santa Fé in what is now New Mexico. Santa Fé was a city of Mexican culture. Major Pike had lived most of his life in an English culture.

Zebulon Pike was pleased with some of the things he saw. They fit his ideas of what was right and what was proper. Other activities did not please him. They went against the ideas that he valued. He had learned his ideas in an English culture. He was less familiar with the Mexican culture. Some of the sights and customs he observed in Santa Fé were pleasant to him, while others were unpleasant.

He found the Mexicans to be polite and well-mannered. He was treated with grace and courtesy and entertained in a fine manner. He appreciated this kind of treatment and commented upon it in his journal.

He described the life of Mexican women in detail. He thought that they were kept within their houses against their will. He felt that they were allowed less freedom than the Mexican men and that they did not take an interest in politics. Major Pike was not in favor of this treatment and said so in his journal.

The major did not approve of the religious ways of the Mexican people. Their religious ideas were different from his own. He felt that the Catholic church of the Mexicans was the cause of many superstitions among the people. Major Pike was a Protestant, and his church had broken away from the Catholic church many years earlier. There were still angry feelings between the two religious groups.

PROBLEM NUMBER ONE: HOW CAN WRITTEN HISTORY AFFECT FEELINGS?

69

Major Pike was amazed at some of the Mexican ways of recreation. He was particularly disturbed by the dancing. The Mexicans were very fond of the fandango, a dance that was brought to the Southwest by the men from Mexico. The women in the dance wore bright and colorful dresses. The costumes were full and fitted loosely. The dancing was gay, and the women danced with joy and with skill.

Dancing was not popular among Major Pike's friends in the East. Their background was more quiet, and their recreation was more likely to follow a pattern that favored reading and conversation. Major Pike frowned upon such dancing and said so in his journal.

We can judge the effect of Major Pike's journal by thinking about that time in history. Try to answer these questions about his report:

---

1. Do you think Major Pike's judgments are based upon facts or upon opinions? In what ways?
2. What might people who read the Pike journal have thought about the people of New Mexico?
3. How might the writings of Major Pike have affected the course of history in the Southwest?
4. How could Major Pike have found out more about the Mexican culture before he wrote his account?
5. Would differences between the people of New England and of the Southwest keep them from being friends? How?
6. How do misunderstandings between people get started? Why do they continue?

Dancing was very popular among the people of the Southwest

We can now look at two imaginary case studies to get a better understanding of how Major Pike might have arrived at some of his opinions. One study will describe the kind of world in which the major might have lived. The other study will describe the kind of world which he visited.

CASE STUDY

I am James Smith of Salem, Massachusetts. My town was settled in 1626. It is a well-known seaport on the shores of the Atlantic Ocean. It was a haven for privateers during both the Revolutionary War and the War of 1812. Most of the people here have an English background.

The weather in my area is often damp and cold. It rains a great deal. The rain makes everything green for most of the year. There are many pastures and ponds and rivers around the town. The most beautiful pond, Spring Pond, is southwest of the town.

Most of the buildings in Salem are made of wood. The many churches are simple and undecorated. Decorations of any kind are frowned upon by the townspeople.

Business is looked upon with favor. Business houses are closed only on the Sabbath. A business man is honored for his success.

We do not like games of chance. The use of cards and dice is considered to be unwelcome behavior. Amusements that depend upon chance are liked by few of my neighbors.

Occasionally, there are great parties. They are held either in the Assembly House or in Hamilton Hall. The best people are invited. The guests are orderly, and their behavior is formal.

VIEW OF SALEM, MASSACHUSETTS.

I am José Galván of Santa Fé, New Mexico. My town was settled in 1610. It is in a mountain valley almost 7,000 feet above sea level. The town is the capital of the Mexican province of New Mexico. The citizens of the town are from many backgrounds. They are Indians, Spaniards, and mestizos, a mixture of Spanish and Indian ancestors. All of the people are Mexican citizens.

The life of the people centers around the churches. The churches are decorated in bright colors and are built of adobe, a clay found nearby. Flowers are brought to the churches on Sundays and on special holidays. Holidays also bring High Masses, singing, and the burning of incense.

Most of the people of the town farm the surrounding lands, but there are other ways of earning a living. The working people look forward to the holidays when they can get together and have fun. At the Plaza, people dance, sing songs, and play guitars. Some people enjoy card playing and dice throwing.

Once a year, we all go to the fair at Taos. There we can barter for new goods and enjoy the festivities. Talk at these annual gatherings is mostly about horses and politics.

1. How are the lives of these two boys alike?

2. How are their lives different?

3. Which differences do you see that might cause clashes between them?

4. Do you see the ways in which the boys could avoid such clashes?

5. What would you predict might happen if a boy from Salem today went to Santa Fé?

6. What might happen if a boy of today's Santa Fé moved to Salem?

7. If problems were to happen, would they be like the problems of long ago?

View of street in Santa Fé, New Mexico

SLANTED HISTORY AS A BARRIER

Attitudes can be formed in many ways. One of these ways is through the study of history. The printed word is very powerful. We too often believe what we see in print without checking whether it is fact or opinion.

In the history of the United States and of Mexico, there have been clashes and fights, conflicts and wars. The stories of these battles depend upon whether you are going to school in Mexico or in the United States. Your reaction to the stories depends upon whether you are American or Mexican. In many American history books, the Mexican is the enemy. In many Mexican books, the American is the enemy.

The following episodes took place between the two countries. They demonstrate the ways in which history can be used to build patriotism.

HISTORICAL COMPARISON

The gringos invaded Mexico's sacred soil in 1846. Under General Zachary Taylor and Winfield Scott, untold horrors were committed. Mexico was very unfortunate. It had a general, Santa Anna, who was probably in the pay of the American government. He did not properly defend Mexico City.

However, there is an episode in the war which shows the bravery of the Mexicans. In spite of the fact that they were poorly equipped, the Mexicans did fight back. At Chapultepec Castle, six boys held off the whole American army. The boys, some of them not yet fifteen years old, were cadets at the military school. When they had no more to fight with, they wrapped themselves in the Mexican flag and threw themselves from a cliff, yelling "Viva, Mexico!"

76

HISTORICAL COMPARISON

One of the most glorious victories in the history of Texas was the Battle of the Alamo. It was fought on March 6, 1836. It took place in a fort that was once a Spanish mission. Bill Travis and one hundred fifty men stood off thousands of Mexicans led by General Santa Anna. The battle gave Sam Houston more time to gather his valiant forces for the fight for Texas independence.

The Mexicans savagely massacred all the heroic Texans. They shot all the prisoners. The Texans had the last word, however. With the cry of "Remember the Alamo," democracy came to Texas.

1. In which country's history books might each of the stories have appeared?

2. If you were Mexican American and read about the Alamo only, how would you feel?

3. If you were an Anglo-American and read about Los Niños Heroes only, how would you feel?

4. What would be a fair way for a teacher in either country to present these historical events?

5. How can you tell that the person who wrote each account was trying to reach the patriotic feelings of his readers?

6. What are the problems that a historian might have in writing about events of the past?

7. Write a fair account of a recent fight on your schoolyard.

The Alamo

Davy Crockett is depicted among the fighters at the Alamo   WALT DISNEY PRODUCTIONS

The people who write accounts of the past sometimes tell what they see from their own point of view. Some of the accounts have been written without understanding the reasons behind the activities they are reporting. When all of the facts are not reported, bad feelings can result. These feelings can be passed on to future generations if the accounts are not corrected.

We need also to understand the customs of other people. Some of these customs cannot be changed without someone suffering deeply. Strong religious beliefs can be difficult to change. So can ideas about what is right and what is wrong. People with such deep beliefs may hold on to them regardless of the penalty.

SUMMARY

University of New Mexico, Albuquerque

CHAPTER 4

What Are The Barriers To Progress?

Mexicans lived in the southwestern part of our country for hundreds of years before the coming of the American. They mixed with the Indians and settled in what is today called the Southwest. There were already churches, schools, and villages here when the Anglo-Americans first came.

Before 1848, the Southwest was Mexico's Northwest. After that time, the region became part of the United States. Attempts were made to Americanize the people, but they resisted. They retained their language, their culture, and their religion.

THE AMERICAN SOUTHWEST

---

1. How does it help to know about the contributions of the Mexicans to the United States?

2. How could knowing this bring a better self-image to people of Mexican descent?

Three groups of people in the United States have not wanted to become Americanized. These resisting groups are the Mexican American, the French-Canadian, and the American Indian. Each of them has wanted to keep the individual differences of its own culture.

Within each of these groups, however, certain members have wanted to become Americanized. They have wanted to become more like the majority of Americans. Such people speak only English and follow American patterns of living. They often move to neighborhoods where other English-speaking Americans live.

People within these three groups have a great respect for education. They have wanted their children to learn the basic skills and attitudes that help a culture to progress. Most schools in this country, however, have been set up to teach within the Anglo-American culture.

The Anglo-American culture is the culture of the majority of the people in the country. The majority wants the schools to teach the English language and the ways to act in an Anglo-American culture. The public schools find it difficult to meet the needs of the people in the three groups that prefer not to become Americanized.

The Mexican American traces his ancestors to our neighbor on the south, Mexico. When Mexico broke away from Spain, it became a divided country. Today, it is one of the leading nations of the Americas. Since 1910, it has shifted its course to become a modern nation. There are still poor farmers in Mexico, but industry is also booming there. The country is a leader in the manufacture of prefabricated schoolhouses. It is considered to be the cultural capital of Latin America. Education has been so successful that most of the people, particularly in the cities, are able to read and write.

---

1. Does this picture of Mexico change your image of that country?
2. What might this picture do to the stereotype that all Mexicans are lazy?

Newcomers from Mexico have continued to come into the Southwest. This constant movement has helped to keep the Mexican American culture different from that of the Anglo-American majority.

---

1. If you lived in a Mexican-American town near the border of the United States and Mexico, would you need to know English?

2. Would you find any customs of the average American school in conflict with your own way of life?

3. If you were proud of your Mexican ancestors, what kinds of subjects would you want taught in school?

4. Would there be an advantage in knowing two languages?

5. Would there be good reasons for being part of and understanding two cultures?

ABOUT THE FRENCH-CANADIANS

Historians believe that there are many similarities between the French-Canadians and the Mexican Americans. The French settled in Canada in much the same way as the Spanish settled in the Southwest. They did not borrow as much from the Indians as the Spanish did. The French, instead, brought their culture and their language to Canada.

From Quebec, the capital city of the French-Canadian empire, they spread through eastern Canada and into New England. In 1763, following the war between the French and the English, Canada became part of the British Empire. The French-Canadians were now ruled by people of an English-speaking culture. Efforts were made to make them follow the English way of life. The French-Canadians resisted these efforts and struggled to keep their own culture.

86

Quebec remains the capital of the French-Canadian empire

In their struggle, the French-Canadians developed a culture which was not French, not Canadian, and not English. The new culture is unique. They act and think differently from the French in France and the English-speaking Canadians. The French-Canadians are proud of this difference and try to protect it from being changed.

Their resistance to change has helped these people to keep their culture and their language. Some of them think that the English-speaking majority are intruders. They think that those who want them to change are foreigners. Most French-Canadian, though, simply feel that they are not in the mainstream of Canadian life, and they prefer it that way.

Today, several million French-Canadians live in the United States. Even in New England, many resist being forced to take part in an Anglo-American culture. They like to listen to the French language programs from Montreal in Canada, their old home. They remain Catholics, and they celebrate the same church holidays as they did in Canada. In all ways, they try to hold on to their old ways, the ways that they like the best.

---

1. Why do you think that the French-Canadians feel so strongly about keeping their own culture?

2. How do you think it feels to believe that you are one of a conquered people?

3. In New England, should English, French, or both languages be taught to French-Canadian children? Why?

The first people to settle in the Americas were the Indians. At one time there were about one million Indians north of the Rio Grande River. Today, there are less than 700,000 in the same area.

The American Indian had his own culture, his own language, and his own values. He developed his way of life long before the white man came to his lands. The Indian family members had strong ties to one another, and they passed on the Indian way of life from generation to generation. He had strong beliefs which he did not want to change.

ABOUT THE
AMERICAN
INDIAN

Southwest Indians display their colorful costumes, although today most dress in modern clothing

When the white men first came through their lands, the Indians were helpful to them. They soon changed their minds. Force and pressure were used to take land from the Indians. The Indians resisted, fought back, and made war upon the men who had become their enemies.

Today, the Indian has lost most of his lands. He and his fellow Indians live, for the most part, on reservations. Many, however, have moved to the city to find jobs. In the city, the Indians usually group themselves together. The American Indian is not in the mainstream of American society. He shares this problem with the Mexican American and other minority groups.

---

1. Why do most Indians live on reservations?
2. What problems does the Indian have when he moves to the city?
3. From what you already know, could you decide what subjects the Indian would like taught in school?
4. How could you get more information about the American Indian?
5. How could you judge whether your information was true?
6. What are some stereotypes about Indians?

A NEGATIVE SELF-IMAGE

One of the best ways to become successful is to copy from a successful person. Sometimes we do not have examples of successful people that we can copy. Without such good models, we can have few hopes of becoming successful people ourselves.

Many of you have seen western movies. You will remember the ones that pictured cowboys and Indians. Keep those in mind as you try to answer the next group of questions.

1. If you were an American Indian, how would you feel about seeing picture after picture in which the Indian is always the "bad guy" and always loses?

2. Would you feel you were like the Indians in the movies?

3. Did they look the way you do now?

4. Would you be discouraged? Angry? Embarrassed? Confused?

5. Would you be inspired to model yourself after these Indians?

6. Is that the way it really happened?

7. Why are the endings of such movies usually bad for the Indian?

Richard was raised on an Indian reservation. His family follows many ancient Indian customs. His father has taught him that when a person points his finger at another person, he puts an evil sign on that person. All the members of Richard's family believe this superstition. Richard's teacher keeps on pointing at him.

1. Why is Richard uncomfortable when the teacher points at him?
2. How could Richard change his feelings about the teacher's habit?
3. How could the teacher help Richard?

The following case studies describe some other examples of negative self-images. Read them to build your knowledge of this problem. Answer the questions thoughtfully.

The teacher has asked the members of the class to make reports about the contributions of various minority groups. The reports are to be based upon recent television programs. This is the report that Bill Brown wrote about the Mexican American:

I chose the Mexican American to write about. I know they have contributed many things. However, I saw few Mexican American stars on television. There is not one show about these people. In fact, the only thing I saw on T.V. was a commercial. Aside from that, I know that the Mexican American has contributed the taco and the tortilla.

1. Would you get the same impression if you were Bill Brown?
2. If you were a Mexican American, how would you feel if you did not see Mexican Americans on television?
3. If you were a Mexican American, how would you feel if someone called you a "taco"?

Mr. Lewis, a teacher, has called ten-year-old Francisco into his room after school. He says, "Francisco, you are not doing well in your work. You should study harder. Sometimes I feel that you know what to put down on tests, but you do not try. That is a bad habit. You will need your education later on in your life."

Francisco replies, "Why should I study, Mr. Lewis? I can't be a teacher like you. I can't be an astronaut, either. There are no Mexican American astronauts."

1. How many Mexican American teachers do you think there were at Francisco's school?

93

2. How many Mexican American principals do you think he has seen?

3. Why is Francisco so sure he can never become an astronaut?

4. Do you think that Francisco has read about many successful Mexican Americans?

5. Is Francisco right when he says it is useless to study? Why?

6. How would you answer him if you were the teacher?

CASE STUDY

Reynaldo's father wears his hair long. He also has a moustache. Rey loves and respects his father. Like many Mexican American boys, he wants to be like his father. The principal of his school orders Rey to cut his hair. He tells Rey that long hair makes him look like a hoodlum.

1. Why might it be difficult for Rey to cut his hair?

2. If you were Rey's father, what might you say to the principal?

3. If you were the principal, how might you convince Rey to cut his hair?

Progress for Mexican Americans has been slowed by these barriers:

SUMMARY

1. The desire of minority groups to keep the individual differences of their cultures.

2. A negative self-image caused by a lack of successful models.

True facts need to be presented, rather than distortions and half-truths. Only then can we recognize the problems faced by minorities that are in a society that is foreign to them.

CHAPTER 5

How Do
Living Conditions Change?

In the early history of the United States, people from other countries came here in groups. Some of these immigrants chose to live in cities rather than in the country. They usually chose the part of a city where other people from their home country lived.

Some immigrants came into the United States from Mexico. They settled in the Southwest where there were other people from their home country. The parts of the city where the Mexican Americans chose to settle is called a "barrio." The word "barrio" means neighborhood.

In the barrio, Mexican Americans feel safe from culture clash. They speak Spanish, and they follow their own way of life. They do not need to follow English ways, and so they feel comfortable. While it is true that many poor people live in the barrio and that there are many older houses there, the barrio is not a slum.

THE BARRIO

---

1. What would be the advantages of living in a barrio?
2. What would be the disadvantages?
3. Do all Mexican Americans live in barrios?
4. How could you find out where other Mexican Americans live?

97

Mexican Americans preserve their way of life in the barrio.

The word "ghetto" is sometimes confused with the word "barrio." They are alike in some ways, but they are not identical.

THE GHETTO

Ghettos were formed by immigrants. They chose to live in a part of a city where there were other people like themselves. In the ghetto, they could keep the ways of the "old country." They could continue to speak the language of the country from which they came.

As the children of the ghetto went to school, they learned the English language and the English way of life. They began to drop some of the old customs. When the children were old enough, they moved away from the ghetto. As children began to move away, the ghetto began to lose some of the cultural differences that had set it apart from the rest of the city.

98

The Mexican Americans within the barrio like to keep most of their cultural differences. Their children are likely to stay in the barrio. The cultural differences that remain bring a certain richness and beauty to the whole city. When these differences are lost, everybody becomes much like everyone else. The city, and the country, lose something precious.

---

1. Why might most immigrants have settled in ghettos?
2. What are the differences between a ghetto and a barrio?
3. Describe a ghetto in your own words.
4. What are the advantages and disadvantages of living in barrios and ghettos?

THE BORDER PULL

You may wonder why the barrio is able to keep its cultural differences better than the ghetto. One reason is the "border pull." Mexicans have been coming north into the United States for a long time. This constant flow of Mexican immigrants into this country has helped the cultural differences to remain. There are always new people coming in who keep the old ways.

We can look at some facts about immigration to see how the closeness of the Mexican border has made a difference. Mexico is greatly influenced by the United States; the border region of the United States is influenced by Mexico. Both countries have to make cultural adjustments to one

99

**TOTAL IMMIGRATION
TO UNITED STATES
BETWEEN 1820
AND THE PRESENT.**

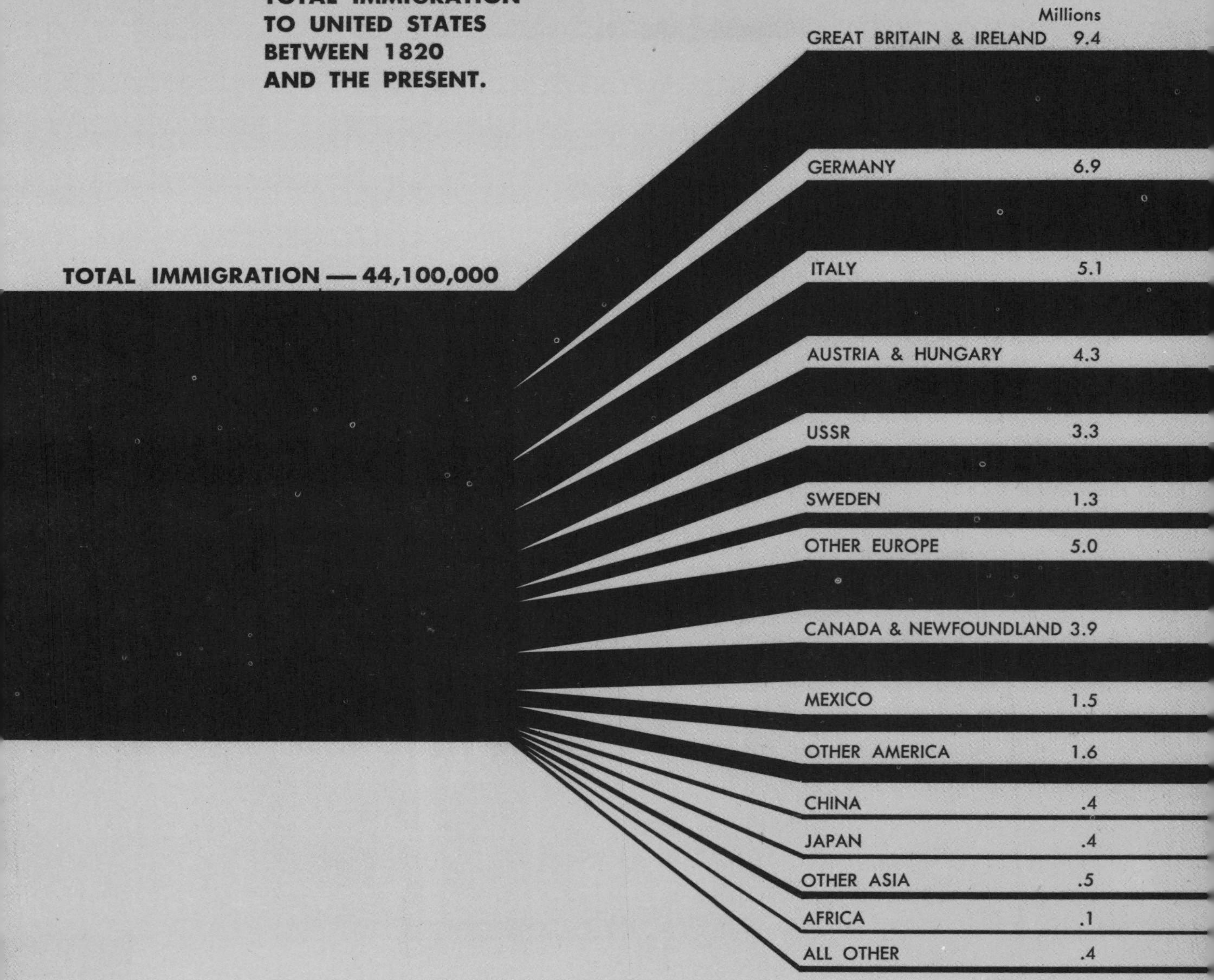

Millions

GREAT BRITAIN & IRELAND   9.4

TOTAL IMMIGRATION — 44,100,000

GERMANY   6.9

ITALY   5.1

AUSTRIA & HUNGARY   4.3

USSR   3.3

SWEDEN   1.3

OTHER EUROPE   5.0

CANADA & NEWFOUNDLAND 3.9

MEXICO   1.5

OTHER AMERICA   1.6

CHINA   .4

JAPAN   .4

OTHER ASIA   .5

AFRICA   .1

ALL OTHER   .4

another. The closer one lives to the border, the greater is the influence of the other country and the greater is the need for adjustments. The farther one lives from the border, the less important the pull becomes.

The barrio serves the needs of Mexican Americans in helping them retain their culture

We can look at four different barrios in the United States to see how the border pull influences the way of life.

Crystal City, Texas, is the winter garden of the state. It is known as the "Spinach Capital of the World." A large statue of Popeye hovers over the city. It is close to the Rio Grande Valley in the southeastern part of the state. The area around the city has always been mostly Mexican American.

Most of the residents of Crystal City are Mexican Americans. They work in the fields, in the canneries, and in other industries. Most of the truck farms, the factories, and the businesses are owned by Anglo-Americans. Most of the Mexican Americans continue to speak Spanish, and over eighty percent of the residents conduct their daily affairs in that language. They have kept much of their culture the same as it has been for many years.

Farming is an important part of the economic life of Crystal City, Texas

Stores of many kinds are found in the barrio of East Los Angeles

Los Angeles, California, was first settled by people who came north from Mexico. Located little more than one hundred miles from the border with Mexico, it is a city of about three million people. Most of the residents are English-speaking.

There are more people of Mexican descent in Los Angeles than in any other city in the world, with two exceptions. Only Mexico City and Monterrey in Mexico have a greater number. Over 300,000 Mexican Americans live in the barrio of East Los Angeles. Many people have lived in the barrio for as long as four generations. The Mexican culture has been kept strong, strengthened by a large number of immigrants from Mexico each year. There are, however, strong Anglo-American influences.

103

Albuquerque, New Mexico, is a city with a wonderful climate. The city is the commercial center of New Mexico. The present city was founded in 1706 on the site of an Indian village.

Until recently, the people of the city were mostly Spanish-speaking. In recent years, many Anglo-Americans have moved here. They now outnumber the Spanish-speaking people four to one.

Albuquerque has also become the home of the University of New Mexico. Students come from all over the United States to study here. The city still has strong cultural ties with Mexico, but the ties are becoming weaker.

Educational needs are served by the University of New Mexico in Albuquerque

Chicago, Illinois, is the home of many thousands of Mexican Americans

Chicago, Illinois, is hundreds of miles from Mexico, the furthest away of the four barrios. Streams of immigrants have come here from Mexico seeking work. They have come to the factories of Chicago, as well as those of Kansas City, Detroit, and Milwaukee. Nearby East Chicago, Indiana, is one of the great urban-industrial areas of the world.

People in this region are largely employed in manufacturing, both light and heavy. In 1960, there were more than 68,000 Mexican Americans in Chicago. There were more than 6,000 in East Chicago, as well as 3,000 Puerto Ricans and other minority groups.

The Mexican immigration to Chicago started fifty years ago. The first and second generations of the immigrants stayed together in the barrio. By the third generation, however, things began to change. The children did not feel as strongly as their parents that the barrio was important. They did not feel the need to keep their Mexican identity. This struggle for identity is still going on, and the pressures to leave the barrio become greater each year.

105

THE PROBLEM OF URBAN-IZATION

More and more people in the United States are moving from the country into the city. Forty years ago, eight of every ten Mexican Americans could be found in the country, or rural, areas. Today, eight out of ten are found in the city, mostly in the barrios. Between 1950 and 1960, the number of Mexican Americans in the United States doubled. This means that the number of Mexican Americans in the city barrios has doubled and that the cities and the barrios have become very crowded. Under these conditions, problems begin to arise.

Let's look at the life of one migrant farm worker and his family to help us to understand.

CASE STUDY

Paco Martínez and his family travel to California every May to harvest the crops. The Martínez family moves many times and works on many farms. They live in many houses as they move from farm to farm. In late October, the family returns to its own home in southeast Texas. Migrant farm work has added over two thousand dollars to the family income. For the rest of the year, the father is a handyman, and the mother is a maid.

1. What problems will the family have during the time it is harvesting crops?
2. How would you feel as a member of the Martínez family?
3. Why do you think they do the kind of work that they do?
4. What problems might the children in the family have in school?

Many families, like the Martínez family, are moving from the country to the cities. Machines are doing many of the jobs that the family members used to do. Many of these people want better educational opportunities for their children. Others want a better job or more money. They move to the barrios of such cities as Los Angeles or San Diego, California; Phoenix, Arizona; San Antonio or Dallas, Texas; and Detroit, Michigan.

In the cities, the families must face problems. The kinds of problems will become clearer in the next case study.

Manuel López and his family live in the city. The family has a very difficult time finding a place in which to live. The mother, Gloria, needs to find a job. Things are very expensive in the city. Manuel works at night, and the children stay with a neighbor.

CASE STUDY

1. What do you think will be the family's first reaction to the city?
2. Why might the family have a difficult time finding a place in which to live?
3. Why might the barrio be the most likely place in which to look for a house?
4. If you were one of the family members, what changes in your life might you feel most strongly?
5. What happens to a family's security in situations like this?

Over the last forty years, many Mexican American families have had to make the same kinds of adjustments as did the López family. Like most Americans, they have had to meet the problems of urbanization. Jobs become scarce, especially for the untrained person. Added to the problems of finding a house and a job, the heads of families may need to be retrained for new skills.

In the meantime, the families like the López family can take root in the barrios. For a time, they can preserve the customs with which they are familiar. They can feel more secure as they begin to deal with their problems. And the problems come quickly and often.

TECHNOLOGY CAUSES PROBLEMS

Barrios are usually found near the center of the city. In these areas, older houses can be rented at low rents. In many cities, the old plazas were in the center of the city. Here, during the day, people gathered to talk, to gossip, to buy, and to sell.

As cities grow, the property near the center often becomes very valuable. People want this central property for office buildings and for high-rise apartments. Sometimes the barrio stands in the way of the changes that people want to make. People then say that the barrio is old and that it is an eyesore. They say that the barrio does not give the city a good image, and they demand that it be torn down.

URBAN RENEWAL

Older, run-down property near the center of a city is often purchased and the buildings on it torn down. New buildings and apartments can be built on the land in place of the older structures. These changes are called urban renewal. The name comes from the claim that the older area is being renewed with newer and more modern buildings. In some people's minds, urban renewal is a sign of progress. In the minds of other people, such changes are not

110

progress at all. When the older buildings are sold, the people living in them cannot afford to live in the new apartments. They must move to another area. Forcing people to move can cause hardships and other problems.

Older homes near the center of the city are razed in the Bunker Hill area in Los Angeles

1. What happens to the people who must move from their property?

2. Imagine that a man in the barrio paid $9,000 for his home and needs to move away. Homes in other areas cost $25,000. What are his choices for a place in which to live?

3. Do you think he can find a home to replace the one that is being torn down? Will it be as good a house? Will it cost about the same?

When a section of the city is renewed, the rents are usually higher than they had been. The family which once paid $75 a month for rent cannot afford the $250 a month rents in the new buildings. The fathers of the families cannot find jobs that pay enough to enable them to pay the higher prices.

New high-rise apartments, Bunker Hill Towers, are built on the expensive central-city land

Sometimes, people are forced to move away from the barrios because the property is being rezoned. Land once zoned for homes is rezoned to be used for factories or apartments. As a rule, rezoned land is worth more money. Speculators, who are buyers that hope to make a great deal of money from their property, buy the rezoned land. They hold it until they can get the highest possible price. Sometimes the value of the land goes up, and sometimes it goes down. The speculator sometimes makes the money he hoped for, and sometimes he loses his investment. Speculators are sometimes called "absentee landlords."

During the time that an absentee landlord holds the property, he rents the buildings on it to people in need of a place to live. Such landlords often do not repair or repaint the buildings they own. They do not wish to invest additional money in property they soon hope to sell.

When an area is rezoned, factories may be built on land that once held homes. The new factories may surround homes in neighboring areas. Business may be built to serve the factory workers. Grocery and department stores, too, may intrude into residential areas.

---

1. If a landlord does not care about his property, will his tenant be likely to care for it?
2. Over the years, what might happen to the house on such rezoned land?
3. How will changing conditions affect the children who are growing up in the area?
4. How might the pride of the residents in their neighborhood be rebuilt?

CHANGES FOR FREEWAYS

People are often forced to move away from the center of large cities. They move to the suburbs, the areas that surround the city. Freeways are built to connect the suburbs to one another and to the city. The city's center may become the crossroad for many freeways. Some of the freeways may pass through the barrios, and the houses will be torn down for freeway construction. Many people will be uprooted to make way for these highways.

There is constant noise and dirt during the process of freeway construction. Nearby homes can become dusty and uncomfortable. More and more people are likely to move out to look for more pleasant living conditions.

Freeways may also take away the green areas near the city's center. A lack of parks and recreational areas may become a serious problem. Such a problem occurred in the barrio of East Los Angeles in California.

Hollenbeck Park had been built in East Los Angeles by German immigrants. The German Jews who built it wanted it to look just like the parks back home in Germany. The Mexican Americans who later moved into the area loved the park. It became a center for much barrio activity. When a freeway was built through East Los Angeles, it passed through the middle of the park. What were once beautiful gardens became places of concrete and raw earth.

---

1. Why are parks needed in crowded cities?
2. Where might people go for recreation when there are no parks?
3. Why is it important to have green areas in the center of a city?
4. Why might a lack of parks contribute to other city problems?

114

The freeway crosses over Hollenbeck Park

A barrio is a part of a city where many Mexican Americans live. Within the barrio, the people speak Spanish and follow the way of life of the Mexican culture. The flow of immigrants from Mexico helps to keep the Mexican influence strong. Many Mexican Americans want to keep their cultural differences. They often stay within the barrios to follow this way of life.

The ghetto, too, is a part of the city settled by one particular group of people. The ghetto, however, allows more cultural changes to take place from outside influences. Both the ghetto and the barrio give people who have recently arrived in this country a secure feeling. They might not have this security in any other part of the city.

Today, more people are moving into the cities. They come for better jobs, better education, better homes, and a better way of life. New families crowd into already crowded areas. Space becomes scarce, and people face new problems.

Sometimes, the barrio is the only place in which a Mexican American can afford to live. Barrios are often near the centers of cities. Property in the barrio becomes more and more valuable as people decide to build high-rise apartment and office buildings. Barrio families are often forced to move out.

Freeway construction causes many changes in the cities. Parks and other recreational areas are destroyed. Homes may be torn down and the tenants forced to move. Rezoning can cause the same kinds of damage. Factories and businesses can surround homes that were once lovely residential areas.

SUMMARY

117

The young Chicanos shown here campaigning are participating in the democratic ways of government.

CHAPTER 6

Where Is The Mexican American In Today's Society?

In an earlier chapter, you learned that the states of California, Arizona, New Mexico, and Texas are called the American Southwest. You learned also that the Southwest was once the property of Mexico and that Mexicans settled there long before the Anglo-American came. When the Southwest became a part of the United States, the descendants of these Mexicans continued to live there. As the Anglo-Americans moved westward, the Mexican Americans were outnumbered by them. Today, the Anglo-American is the majority in the Southwest. The Mexican American is one of several minorities.

Other minorities live in this region. A minority is any group of people whose numbers are smaller than those of the majority. The Japanese-Americans are a minority in the Southwest. So are the blacks. The largest minority, however, is still the Mexican American. Out of every 100 people in the Southwest, approximately 12 are Mexican American.

INCOME AND EMPLOYMENT

The Anglo-American family, in 1959, enjoyed a higher average income than did the Mexican American family. The size of the average Anglo-American family was smaller than that of the Mexican American. A careful look at those two facts can reveal that the average income of the Anglo-American is greater than that of the Mexican American. Family is very important to the Mexican American. His family is likely to consist of relatives, such as aunts, uncles, grandmothers, and grandfathers, all living together. This larger idea of family lowers the average income still further.

The amount of income for a family also is affected by the kind of work that people do. There are fewer professionals —doctors, lawyers, dentists, and teachers—among Mexican Americans than among Anglo-Americans. The professions, however, are a goal for many Mexican American students.

The chart on page 121 shows that Mexican Americans do join the ranks of professional people, though not in large numbers. The Mexican American is determined to work to the best of his ability, and this attitude adds to the number of professional people.

The chart also shows the percentages of skilled, semi-skilled, and unskilled workers. Too often it is a true statement that the Mexican American is one of the last to be hired for a job and one of the first to be fired. This factor of unemployment is changing, however. More and more people are impressed with the determination of the Mexican American to overcome the stereotypes that were described earlier in this book.

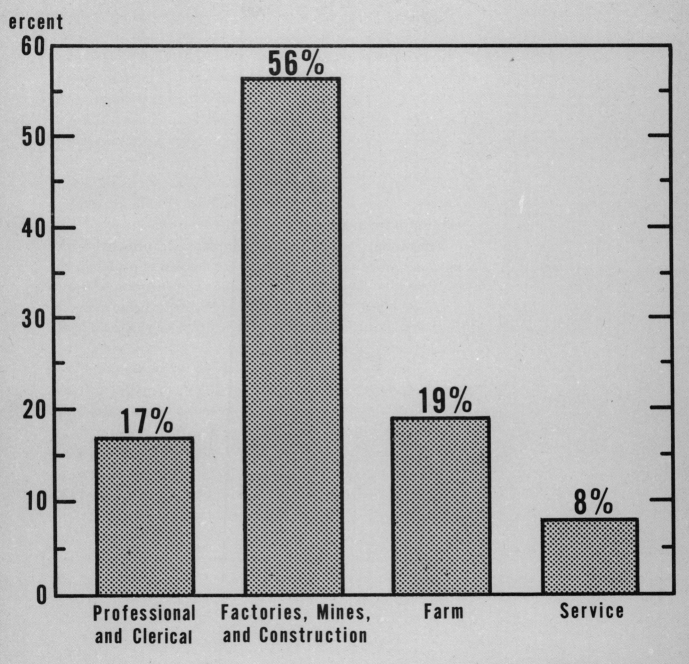

ercent

60

50

40

30

20

17%

10

0

Professional
and Clerical

56%

Factories, Mines,
and Construction

19%

Farm

8%

Service

(1960 Census)

HOUSING

The barrios in the cities contain many older homes. Many of them are in need of major repair. On a housing map, the barrios would show up as tight clusters of homes. The map would show a concentration of Mexican Americans in particular parts of the city. What seems to be needed are more available housing at a rent that can be afforded by these people or a rise in the average income of the minority groups.

POLITICAL REPRESEN- TATION

Since a large part of the population of the Southwest is Mexican American, it would seem proper to find Mexican Americans represented in political offices in ratio with his numbers. This has, however, not been the case. It is true that there have been many Mexican Americans who have served their community and their country in political office, but the number who have served has been far short of the number who might have been able to serve.

It has been said that the Mexican American is apathetic, that he doesn't really care. It has also been said that the Mexican American has been prevented from participating in politics. Without wide participation in the democratic ways of government, the Mexican American does not participate fully in American society.

Another possible reason for the small number of Mexican Americans in politics may be the way cities are divided. The divisions are sometimes made for political reasons. The ways in which the boundaries are drawn can change the political power of a group.

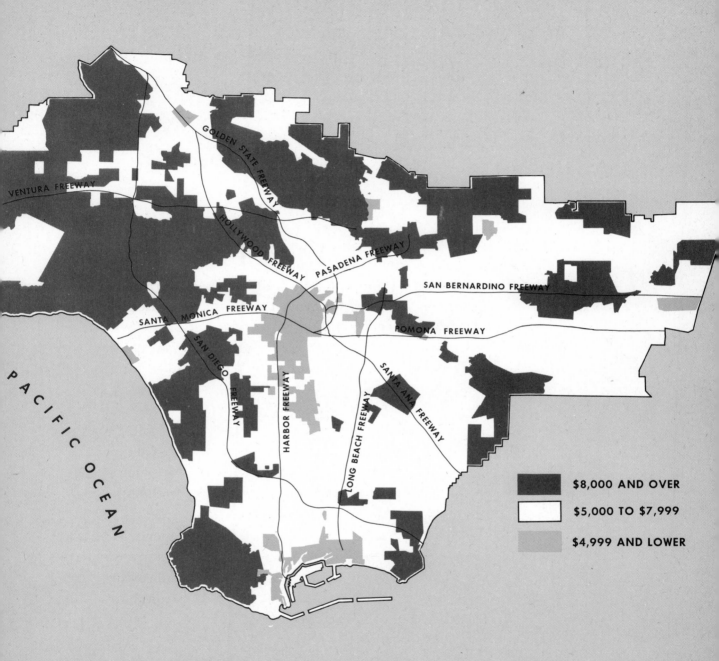

PACIFIC OCEAN

VENTURA FREEWAY

GOLDEN STATE FREEWAY

HOLLYWOOD FREEWAY

PASADENA FREEWAY

SAN BERNARDINO FREEWAY

SANTA MONICA FREEWAY

ROMONA FREEWAY

SAN DIEGO FREEWAY

HARBOR FREEWAY

LONG BEACH FREEWAY

SANTA ANA FREEWAY

$8,000 AND OVER

$5,000 TO $7,999

$4,999 AND LOWER

1. How does the place of the Mexican American in American society compare with that of other Americans?

2. If the facts in this chapter were the only ones that you knew, what would you say is the Mexican American's greatest need?

3. List other needs of the Mexican American in the order of the importance you give them?

Graduating Chicanos realize the need for education

Jobs and income are closely related to education. For various reasons, the educational level of the average Mexican American is below that of most other Americans. Language problems may be one of the reasons for the lower level, and so might the cultural conflict with the Anglo-Americans. A negative self-image may also be considered a reason for the lower level of education.

Cultural conflict may force Mexican Americans to think that the roads to a college education are blocked for them. College training is expensive and the lower income of this group does not often allow money to be spent in this way. Families with many children to support do not always have a free choice of how to spend their money. In the average Mexican American family, when the children are old enough to go to college, they are also old enough to go to work. Their income is needed to allow the family to survive. Mexican American children feel a duty to contribute to their family's income.

It has been said that Mexican Americans do not believe that college is a part of their culture. These same statements add that there is the opportunity, but that the Mexican American does not take advantage of it. What is your reaction to this opinion? Do you think it could be true? How does such a statement fit in with what you have read about stereotyped thinking?

What are the attitudes of the Mexican Americans toward education? Are they affected by the attitudes they may have learned from Mexico? The following case studies may help you to decide.

EDUCATION

Education in Mexico is very important. In 1900, only one of every four Mexicans could read or write. Today, more than seven of every ten, almost three times as many, can do so. Close to 400,000 Mexicans attend the 34 universities and 16 technical institutes in the country.

CASE STUDY

As an example of the growing importance of education, Paco Rubio, 25, is typical of a growing number of young people. His parents had no formal education, but they managed to send him to college. They knew that he would want to attend, because Mexicans value the opportunity to become educated. Mexicans grow up with the desire to attend a college or a university.

As a result of his training, Paco Rubio became an engineer. He was in charge of building Mexico City's Olympic Sports Palace. He was one of the many young Mexicans who took part in planning and carrying out the games and activities for the 1968 Olympic Games. Such people made it one of the most successful Olympic Games to date.

Only a small percentage of Mexican Americans in the United States go to college. Few of them are able to become professional workers. Few of them become teachers or principals. A child growing up in the barrio sees few such Mexican American professionals during his school years. Some people feel that this lack of models, or people to be imitated, slows the Mexican American down.

Professional men offer important models for young people

The 1968 Olympic Games held in Mexico City were a tribute to Mexican education and industry

CASE STUDY

"My name is Luis. I was raised in Pacoima, a suburb in Los Angeles, California. My father was a laborer, and we have many children in the family. When I was sixteen, I dropped out of school to help my family. At that time, there was little effort made to keep me in school. Everyone thought that I would end up as a laborer, anyhow. I never thought of going to college. College is for the rich. Not many Chicanos go to college. I could never have made it, anyhow."

1. Why is there a difference shown in the attitudes of the Mexican and the Mexican American youths?

2. Might it make a difference if the Mexican American student's father were a laborer, a banker, or a lawyer?

3. How do we form our attitudes?

4. Do you think models make a difference in the attitudes of a young person toward education?

Young students crowd the classrooms at San Fernando Valley State College

The Mexican American faces many problems as he tries to get an education. These problems are part of the larger problem of fitting into the modern American society. There seem to be many reasons for the Mexican American to be alienated, or feeling left out. The leaving-out process may begin the day he starts school.

The educational problem is part of a circle. Cultural conflict molds the Mexican American's attitude toward school. The people around him can inspire him or discourage him. If the child is discouraged, he does not go on through school. If he does not go to college, there will be no role images for

SCHOOL
REACTIONS

129

other Mexican American children to imitate. There will be no models upon which other children can base their attitudes.

The following problems may help you in thinking about education for the Mexican American:

PROBLEM NO. 1

Many Mexican American students attend Juanita Junior High School. The school has a Student Council, but the Council does not have a Mexican American member. There are difficulties at the school. Some Mexican American youths act as if they do not care whether or not they come to school.

You are a Mexican American boy at this school. You think you know why these boys and girls dislike school. You believe that the Student Council could help to solve this problem. What action would you take?

PROBLEM NO. 2

You are Juanita Junior High School's principal. You need to hire two teachers for next year. You know about the facts in Problem #1. What qualities would you look for as you interview teachers?

PROBLEM NO. 3

You are a Mexican American girl who has just graduated from Juanita Junior High School. As you enter high school, you find that your counselor has put you into a cooking class. You want to become a teacher. You think that a geography class would be more useful to you than a cooking class. What would you do about this problem?

130

PROBLEM NO. 4

You are a Mexican American farmer. You feel that farmers in your area are not getting a fair price for their crops in the nearby city. You feel that the farmers need someone to speak for them.

There is a position open on the City Council. Someone must be elected to fill that position. You would like to run for the position, but you dropped out of school before you finished high school. What could you do about this problem?

SUMMARY

Mexican Americans are the largest minority group in the Southwest. They are not represented equally in all levels of the American society. Their incomes, on the average, are low. They are often forced to live in run-down houses because of lack of money. There are few Mexican Americans in professional positions in comparison with their numbers. The Mexican American is not often well represented in government. Above all, the education of the average Mexican American is not at a high enough level.

Mexican Americans feel the need to be free of stereo-typed thinking about them. They need successful people from their own culture to become examples for others in the community. They also need to be represented in places where the decisions about them are made.

CHAPTER 7

Do The Problems Have Solutions?

If you have read with thought and with care, you are more aware of the Mexican American people. If you have read this book with a desire to understand it, you are more aware of their problems.

You see the heritage of the Mexican American in many ways and places. The names of many streets and towns are in their native language. You remember their history as you think about the Southwest. You have heard and liked their music, and you may have danced their dances. You are probably familiar with their traditional costumes.

But have you thought about them? Have you thought about the things which you might do to overcome prejudice? Have you considered how you might become more sensitive to their problems? Have you found any ways in which you can help the Mexican Americans and other minority groups take their rightful place in American society.

Five years from now, some of the problems may be solved. If they are, it will be because people like you took action. It will be because sensitive people worked with the Mexican Americans to bring about changes in their living conditions. Everyone has two choices: to care and to help— or to remain silent and turn away.

WHAT CAN BE DONE?

133

UNDERSTANDING THE VALUE OF DIFFERENCES

America is made up of people of all different backgrounds. People talk differently, act differently, dress differently, and have different traditions and values. Some people think that everyone should look, act, and think alike. In this book, we have looked at some of the ways in which people react to differences. We have examined how people might feel if they are different from the majority.

We can review some of the differences the book has mentioned and think of some solutions to the problems that the differences may cause.

Is it wrong to speak another language rather than English? Many schools in the United States have teachers who help children who do not speak English to learn the new language. Some of these boys and girls speak Spanish. Others may speak other languages. Some may speak two or three languages, and they may still not know English. Would it be wrong for you not to speak another language? Perhaps it would be helpful for you to be able to speak your native tongue and another.

Some other people at the schools are trying to help. They are learning Spanish, even though it is not their native tongue. Teachers, counselors, and school secretaries are learning Spanish to be able to talk to people who do not know English. It can make people more comfortable to converse with others who know their language. It is easier to get an idea across in your native language than in a foreign tongue. You feel that people are really trying to understand your problem when they take the trouble to learn your language.

134

What does the future hold for this child?

Is it wrong to dress or to look different? It would be a rather dismal world if everyone was a carbon copy of everyone else. Today, boys and girls of all backgrounds are trying to be themselves. They are protesting the requirements to "do alike" and "be alike." You want to dress the way you want to dress. You want to wear your hair in your own way. You want to express your opinion. If you want to do these things, then you need to look carefully at your attitude toward others.

Do you believe as your family believes? Sometimes, we laugh at the older members of the family when they try to tell us how to act. However, we become angry if anyone else laughs at them. We are angry because these are the things in which we have been taught to believe since childhood. These beliefs may be religious, or they may be traditions handed down through many generations.

In our country, everyone may follow his own beliefs and his own way of living. The only rule is that your way of life must not interfere with the rights and privileges of other people. The customs of other people may seem strange to us. If we look carefully, however, we can learn valuable lessons. We learn why older people are treated with respect in some cultures. We learn why people love their sisters and their brothers so deeply. We can see the reasons for being courteous to strangers. Strange customs can be familiar to us as we open both our eyes and our minds to what happens around us.

Studying the history of many countries shows us that people act differently in different times and in different places. At some times in history, people took unfair actions against foreigners. At other times, they were cruel toward people of different religions. You can be critical of actions such as these. You can suggest better ways in which to act. You can help others to accept the difference in people.

Should you let other people tell you how to act? One of the most important parts of your education has been learning to find solutions to problems. A problem is presented, and you must think of reasonable ways in which it could be solved. You try one idea, change it if you must, and apply it to the problem. If it works, you can apply your solution to other similar problems.

Isn't this the kind of thinking that you can do when you are dealing with people? Perhaps you will hear someone speak in generalizations. If one person is short, isn't everyone of that nationality short? If a person gets angry easily, doesn't everyone of that nationality get angry easily? Apply the ways you are learning to solve problems. You will find that you will look at prejudices in a different way. You will check many sources to find out what really happened in history. You will not be swayed by facts which are not facts at all, but opinions.

KEEPING
AN OPEN
MIND

137

EMPATHIZING WITH OTHER PEOPLE

It is often easy to feel sympathy. We can feel sorry for another person. We can feel sorry that he has no money or that he cannot speak our language. We can feel sorry that his background and his culture are so different that he stands out from the rest of us. Empathy, however, is a different kind of feeling than sympathy. Empathy adds understanding to sympathy and says that it is all right to be different. It says, "I am willing to accept you as you are."

Should everyone live in the same way and in the same places? Some people live in the country, and some people live in the city. Some like apartments, and some prefer houses.

The boys and girls of today are the architects of tomorrow. They are the politicians, the teachers, and the city planners. Your understanding of the things that people need will make you a more successful person. Your education will help you make the decisions about where houses will be built, who will live in these houses, and who will serve these people. Your education—in school, at home, and in the community—will help you to make decisions that will affect the working conditions and the wages of the workers of the future.

The young Chicano and the mature Mexican American represent the future and past in changing cultural ideas

MAKING CHOICES

Solutions to problems may not be easy to find. Certainly some mistakes are going to be made as people try to solve the problems we have been studying. Still, real progress can be made if we are careful about our attitudes. We must be sure that our communities are showing a responsible attitude.

We all make choices about our own attitudes and our own actions. This book has tried to awaken you to the ways in which your attitudes may have been formed and how they will be formed in the future. It has tried to show you that your actions may have been determined by others, even though you may have thought you had been acting on your own. It has not always been easy to understand what has been said. The problem itself is not easy to understand.

Progress depends upon the opportunity to make choices. It depends upon the kinds of choices that people make. In the end, the way we think, feel, and act toward other people depends upon what we know, what we believe, and what we are willing to do.

Each one of us matters.

GLOSSARY

(Page number following each word represents the page on which the word is introduced.)

ancestors, 11   Ancestors are the relatives or members of a family who have lived in past times.

Anglo-American, 14   The term Anglo-American means the people of Anglo-Saxon ancestry who came to America from western Europe, particularly the English. It has come to mean most white people who came to the Southwest.

barrio, 97   A barrio represents a neighborhood or community and is part of a city where Mexican Americans choose to group together.

cartographer, 41   One who works at the science and art of making maps.

case study, 9   A case study is a particular situation in which children or adults act in a certain way.

Chicano, 33   The word Chicano is used to describe a Mexican American.

culture, 11   The educational advancement and historical experiences of people that make up their way of life.

cultural shock, 47   The feeling a person can experience if he is forced to change his way of life.

empathy, 138   Empathy is a feeling of sympathy to which has been added greater understanding.

ghetto, 98   A ghetto is a community or part of the city in which immigrants choose to live and keep the ways of the "old country."

minority, 119   A minority is any group of people whose numbers are smaller than those of the majority in a given area.

stereotype, 37   The term stereotype represents the ideas concerning the characteristics of one person generally given to all people with some of the same characteristics.

surveyor, 40   One who works at finding the contours, measurements and positions of any part of the earth's surface.

sympathy, 138   Sympathy usually includes a feeling of sorrow or sadness.

traditions, 9   Traditions are the beliefs and ideas handed down through a family or a group of people.

veterinarian, 10   A veterinarian is an animal doctor.

INDEX

(m) *map.* (p) *picture.* (ch) *chart.*